MW01122502

for
Amanda, Robin, Alison,
John, Michael, Annemarie and Kirsten
and grandchildren everywhere. R.J.T.

for
My wife Julie and my daughters Leah and Esther.
Thanks to Barbara 'Medici' Sacks, Pegi Williams, Jane Moore,
Sean Moffat, Lyn Stanton and Carolyn Robinson. R.W.S.

Design and Layout:
Rory Stapleton

ISBN 0 947338 60 8

AXIOM

Bill Bilby
and Friends

Verse: Roger Tulloch
Illustrations: Rory Stapleton

Axiom, Australia.

Bill Bilby and the Trilby

Bill Bilby's family heard him say,
"I think I'd like to roam,
To see some other places,
Besides our desert home.

"I'd like to go to Sydney,
Or to Melbourne by the sea:
Maybe have a look at Adelaide.
Yes, that's the life for me."

His mother said, "Well, fancy that!
Go roaming? Well, why not?
But you'd better wear a hat, my boy,
Because the sun's so hot.

"We Bilby's, being night time folk,
Don't travel much by days;
We need something to protect us
From the ultraviolet rays.

"I've got one here. They tell me
That this sort is called a trilby.
It belonged to your great grand-dad,
Alexander James MacBilby."

So she took it from the cupboard,
(From the top shelf by the socks.
To protect it from the desert dust,
It was in a cardboard box.)

It was bluish-grey, a bit like Bill,
And quite soft to the touch.
But when they tried it on him
Those ears were just too much.

They folded them and bent them,
They tied them back with string.
They even plastered them with hair gel,
But that just made them sting.

They pulled and pushed;
                 tried this and that,
Till Bill cried out: "That's enough.
You're giving me a headache.
Why must you be so rough?"

Then taking off his hiking boots,
He lay down on his bed.
He sniffed a disappointed sniff,
And rather sadly, said:

"Please leave me and my ears alone.
I'm never going to roam.
If it means I have to wear a hat,
I'll stay right here, at home."

Salt-Water Crocodile

You should never, never try to smile
At the salt-water crocodile,
Or, if you must, then you should be
So far away that he can't see
Your friendly smile; for this big bloke
Is not like ordinary folk.
(It wouldn't give you any joy
To ask him:"Who's a pretty boy?")

He wears his nose, and two big eyes,
High on his head, so when he lies
And waits for you to take a swim,
He'll see you, but you won't see him.

His skin on top is tough and grey
And white below. Some people say
That's why he's mean and very snappy.
(If you looked like that, would you be happy?)

So, boys and girls, don't waste your smiles
On ugly, mean old crocodiles.

Kookaburra Said To Me

A kookaburra said to me,
While sitting in that old gum tree:
"A wombat is a wondrous thing.
It doesn't dance, it doesn't sing.
Nor drive a car or ride a bike
Or other things that humans like.
But each one has a hairy nose.
Please tell me, have you one of those?"
Before I'd thought of a reply
He laughed out loud and winked one eye,
Then this advice he gave to me.
(I'll pass it on to you. It's free.)
Make sure you never try to take
A photo of a tiger snake.
For though, as snakes, they're not all bad
They have been known to get quite mad
If they should hear the shutter click;
And "Please say cheese!" just makes them sick.
So, if snake photos you MUST take,
Go, try and find a carpet snake,
Because these chaps are much more fun.
(They'll gladly smile for anyone.)

A Wombat is a Wondrous Thing

A wombat is a wondrous thing.
It doesn't read a book, or sing,
Nor drive a car or ride a bike
Or other things that humans like.
But each one has a hairy nose.
Please tell me, have you one of those?

It digs a burrow in the ground
And on hot days that's where it's found
Sheltering from the daytime heat,
Then after dark comes out to eat.
It's brownish-grey and rather fat.
Please tell me, do you look like that?

It looks as though it's pretty slow,
But don't be fooled, for you should know
That when disturbed it runs quite fast
(And if you raced one, you'd come last.)
On all its toes it has strong claws.
Please tell me, have you claws on yours?

Though it sleeps underground, you see
Its cousin sleeps up in a tree.
(Yes, though the thought may make you grin,
Koalas are the wombats' kin.)
But it's aunt is not a kangaroo.
Please tell me, is yours not one, too?

The Mulgara

A mulgara once said to his mate:
"I think it would be really great
To go and live near someone's house
Like any ordinary mouse,
Instead of on these desert plains
Where it hardly ever, ever rains.

I'd live on bread and cheese, or cake.
Or maybe scraps of sirloin steak.
I wouldn't mind a chip or two,
A pizza or some Irish stew;
While buttered bun or creamy rice
I'm sure would be extremely nice.

But I suppose I'm better here
Where we have lived year after year;
Where we can roam beneath the stars
Without dodging bikes or trucks or cars;
Or breathing air that's full of smog.
Where no one has a cat or dog.

No. Fancy foods and all that stuff
Would really not be good enough
For creatures from the desert sand
Who live on bugs and insects and
A grub or two. Yes, just here is nice
For Mulgara (or marsupial mice.)"

The Lyrebird

The Lyrebird's a higher bird
Than any Crow or Friar Bird.
He's also quite a liar bird.
Read on, and you will see.

He can bark like a dog.
He can croak like a frog.
Or make a noise like an axe chopping wood.
Though he can't make a speech,
He can screech a loud screech,
Like the noisiest cockatoo could.

He's a handsome bird, this lyrebird,
Though not much of a flier bird.
And he's very much a shyer bird
Than you see round your yard.

His tail's like a fan
And this show-off bird can
Spread it over his back when he's dancing,
Which he does for his mate.
(She thinks it's just great.
It's the lyrebird way of romancing.)

The Platypus' Duck-Bill

While resting on a rock, one day,
A platypus was heard to say:
"This duck-bill is a handy tool
For finding food down in my pool.
With eyes and ears and nose closed tight,
I feel around there, out of sight,
For juicy worms and bugs to eat,
While swimming with my two front feet.
(My back feet, you might like to know,
I use for steering as I go.)
A duck-bill's great, let me tell you.
I bet you wish you had one, too."

If you chance to see a dolphin

If you chance to see a dolphin when you're going for a swim,
Please smile and nod politely, for it might be my friend Jim,
Who's a very friendly creature, and wears a great big grin
While he plays his underwater games with all his finny kin.

He can talk, oh yes he can, I'm sure you've heard of that,
Though I guess you may have never overheard his sort of chat.
He squeaks and clicks and whistles and makes a quiet sort of moan
He can talk to other dolphins in a language all their own.

He'll play games with human swimmers, and with any passing ship,
But one fish out there in the sea always gives our Jim the pip.
The Sneaky Shark, now there's a fish makes happy dolphins cross,
They'll attack these chaps, and chase them off, to show them
                                                    who's the boss.

So if you're swimming in the sea and dolphins are there too,
You probably won't see a shark, but my advice to you
Is: Make VERY SURE they're dolphins and not sharks you've seen,
Because sharks are often hungry, and when they are they're mean.

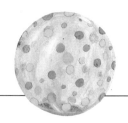

The Emu on Our Coat of Arms

I'm sure all well-read folk have heard
That the emu is a great big bird
That cannot leave the ground at all,
Like other birds, however small.
But, as for knowing how to run
The emu shows you how it's done.
And when it comes to eggs, the Mum
Is just as crafty as they come.
She lays those eggs, all darkly green
(The largest eggs you've ever seen)
In a nest she's trampled on the ground
And then she leaves, just swans around,
While her husband, such a helpful spouse,
Takes over, doesn't growl or grouse
But sits there in the grass and sticks
Until those eggs hatch into chicks.
But for all her faults, her lack of charms,
She's still part of our coat of arms.
(Or is that the male, up there on view
With our heraldic kangaroo?)

Gliders and Spiders

A Great Glider, with a sneer,
Was heard to say, one day last year:
"That girl, Miss Muffet, so they say
Insists on eating curds and whey.
Just why, is quite beyond belief.
She should try eucalyptus leaf
Like all the long-tailed Great Gliders
Who never were afraid of spiders.
Then, instead of running off that day
She could have glided on her way.
Yes, gliding is the way to go,
(It's easier on the feet, you know.)
Please give her this advice from me:
Get breakfast from the old gum tree."
Then, shaking hands—he's so polite—
He swiftly glided out of sight.

Tawny Frogmouth

My friend, Tawny frogmouth, who's a bit like an owl
Said: "I can't whistle or sing. I don't yodel or growl.
I can't sing like the bellbird, who sounds just like a bell,
But I can see in the dark. Can you do that? Pray tell.

I don't give milk like a cow or grow wool like a sheep,
But while they're milking and wooling, and while you're asleep
I catch bugs, frogs and lizards" (his beak gave a 'snap'!)
"As well, I'm a regular flying mouse-trap.

Yes, while you and your family sleep in the night,
I go out hunting, then I snooze while it's light.
But when I'm at home on the branch of my tree,
I can see you—it's easy—but it's hard to see me.

While you try to spot me, I squint shut both my eyes
And stretch myself up straight, and point to the skies.
Then I look like a small branch, or part of a bough.
If you can do that, then please show me how."

So when I agreed that I couldn't do that,
He gave a small smile, then in two seconds flat
He spread both his wings and flew off through the air
To his home in that tree—but I won't tell you where.

Possums on the Roof

It sometimes wakes me with a fright
When, in the middle of the night
The possums from the old gum tree
Jump on my roof. Oh goodness me!
They land on it with such a crash.
Then noisily across they dash
And play the rowdiest of games,
Or call each other nasty names.

Some nights I think they even hold
A jousting match, like knights of old,
Where possums wearing suits of tin
Fight duels, and make a fearful din,
And not content to wear tin suits,
I'm sure they all wear football boots.
(Oh, gosh, why can't their parents choose
To buy them nice, soft tennis shoes?)

And Crusty, he's the dog next door,
Begins to bark and what is more
Wakes all the sleeping girls and boys,
And soon there is a dreadful noise.

If I said please the nicest way,
Do you think they all might go away?

Wally B Wallaby

"Wally B Wallaby, have you ever been
To London, in England, to visit the Queen?"
No, I've not been to England, nor Scotland or Ireland
I've not left my home on Kangaroo Island.

"Wally B Wallaby, then why don't you fly
High up in an aeroplane, up in the sky?"
"Well, I'll tell you:the man has not been born yet
Who can get me, Wal Wallaby, up in a jet."

"Wally B Wallaby, then why don't you swim?
The dolphins and sharks do, and the whale—look at him."
"No way, Mister Lizard. The thought makes me sick.
I once tried to swim, and I float like a brick."

"Wally B Wallaby, you're too much for me.
You won't go by air, and you won't go by sea."
"Well, please go away then and leave me alone.
If you're off to London, then go on your own."

The Black Swan on the River

The koalas are in the old gum tree;
There are Galahs as far as you can see,
The Wedgetail Eagle's flying free,
And the Black Swan's on the river.

The Wombat's on his dusty plain;
The Emu waits and waits for rain;
While Dingoes guard their hot domain,
And the Black Swan's on the river.

The Major Mitchell Cockatoos
Shriek insults at the Big Red 'roos
The Quokkas and the Potoroos
And the Black Swan's on the river.

The Platypus and the Lyrebird
Ask the Echidna: "Have you heard..."
"I know," he snaps, "don't be absurd.
The Black Swan's on the river."

Tasmanian Devils snap and growl.
"Be quiet," says the Boobook Owl.
"Shush!" says the Quoll, with fearsome scowl,
"The Black Swan's on the river."

These creatures, I am sure, agree
It's up to folk like you and me
To make sure that there'll always be
A Black Swan on the river.